SCRIP

# For Everything There Is a Season

## *Ecclesiastes 3:1–8*

ALICE CAMILLE

**Living with Christ** Books

*In thanksgiving for memorable evenings
of conversation with
Megan E. Reilly, Neal P. Fox, David Alex
Mély, Sahil Luthra, and Patrick Heck—
the Brown University brain trust and,
very possibly, the hope of the world*

TWENTY-THIRD PUBLICATIONS
A Division of Bayard
One Montauk Avenue, Suite 200 » New London, CT 06320
(860) 437-3012 or (800) 321-0411
www.23rdpublications.com

ISBN: 978-1-62785-144-2
Library of Congress Control Number: 2015957204
Printed in the U.S.A.

# ❧ CONTENTS ❧

B lame it on The Byrds. They're the folk-rock group who put "Turn! Turn! Turn! (To Everything There Is a Season)" on the charts in late 1965. This made Ecclesiastes Chapter 3 the rare bit of Scripture to burrow deep into the popular consciousness. The Byrds didn't write the song. They generously attributed it to King Solomon of the Bible, claiming it as the #1 hit with the oldest lyrics in the U.S. The song was actually composed by Pete Seeger in the 1950s and recorded a few times before The Byrds got hold of it—and by at least thirty other artists to date, including Judy Collins, Marlene Dietrich, and Dolly Parton. Seeger himself gave away forty-five percent of the royalties, reckoning he deserved credit only for the score and six impassioned words added after the stanza concerning a time for peace: "I swear it's not too late."

These six words by Seeger would point the song squarely into the eyeteeth of the Vietnam War, which was escalating when The Byrds launched their recording. "Turn! Turn! Turn!" became an anthem of the peace movement—which would have been a great surprise to the original author of the text.

So here's the grace, and the dilemma, in undertaking a spiritual exploration of Ecclesiastes 3. Is it possible to get past our singsong acquaintance with this text to grasp it in a new light? Our familiarity with these phrases is as inevitable as it may prove to be inaccurate, or at least inadequate. Now, I'm a Seeger fan; I'd welcome this song at my funeral. But Seeger's reading of the text isn't the only message to be gleaned. And The Byrds' reassuring, almost merry, rendering of the passage misses the author's intent by a mile.

Maybe we can cut a deal at the outset of this book. Let's surrender artistic license to songwriters (and other preachers) to incorporate Scripture into a thesis with its own moral integrity. Scripture is fluid enough to contain multitudes of meanings and to support truth seekers in every generation and context. "Turn! Turn! Turn!" gets a high five for a job well done and mission accomplished. But let's move on to what the writer of Ecclesiastes is getting at.

## OUR CURIOUS GUIDE, QOHELETH

The Book of Ecclesiastes was composed between the third and second centuries BC. King Solomon is an improbable author, having lived centuries earlier. While references to "King David's son" appear in the first two chapters, they quickly disappear as the writer develops his philosophical argument. This doesn't imply that the tribute to King Solomon is a scheme perpetrated by a writer bent on deceiving us. Much Wisdom literature in the Bible is attributed to Solomon, considered the wisest king ever. This literary homage can be compared with that of modern screenwriters who extend the adventures of Sherlock Holmes to admit new episodes that were clearly not composed by Sir Arthur Conan Doyle, who died in 1930. We all know Conan Doyle didn't write this new stuff. But the fun is in pretending that Sherlock Holmes and Dr. Watson go on forever with new villains to foil

3

and crimes to solve. In a similar way, for Wisdom writers, Solomon rules and philosophizes on.

So who did write Ecclesiastes? As with many biblical works, we don't have a name, but we do have a profile. This period of history saw Greece in charge of the region in and around Israel. Greek influence pervaded every aspect of life, and the impact of the Greek philosophical tradition was felt by scholars of Israel. The final centuries before the time of Jesus fostered wisdom texts as teacherly as Ecclesiastes and Sirach; as adventuresome as Tobit and Judith; as well as the shining literary highlight of the Book of Wisdom.

The writer of Ecclesiastes presents himself simply as Qoheleth (koe-HELL-eth), which means "the assembler." Either this fellow called assemblies to gather, or he gathered and assembled ideas.

The claim that Solomon authored Ecclesiastes, then, is for The Byrds. The band is probably safe in claiming their hit song as having the oldest lyrics in the U.S., nonetheless. Wrong author, and six or seven centuries later than suggested, it still beats most chart-topping tunes by a couple solid millennia.

## WHAT'S THE MESSAGE?

Scholars distill Qoheleth's message to a single question posed in chapter one: What are earthly projects worth at the end of a lifetime? Qoheleth frames his reply with shocking brevity: nothing! The Hebrew word employed repeatedly in the book is *hebel*, usually translated "vanity" or "emptiness." *The Jewish Study Bible* renders hebel as futility. The ever-jaunty *Message Bible* prefers smoke. As in: everything you care about right now is bound to go up in it.

We may feel just a little offended at this idea. Are our sometimes heroic investments in family life nothing? Could our efforts at becoming educated, thoughtful, informed citizens be an utter waste of time? Is human labor and community-building, politics and nation-building, religion, commerce, art, and love just "chasing after wind"? If the work of our hands across a lifetime is an empty pursuit, would we do just as well burrowing into the couch and binge-watching our shows?

If you feel dismayed at the suggestion, then you're right where Qoheleth expects his audience to be. He's an old fellow who's worked hard and built an empire of sorts: family, possessions, land, reputation, and career. But more than an acquirer of property and a proud résumé, Qoheleth has been diligent with self-development too. He's learned, cultured, and evolved. He's done his "inner work." He's taken the spiritual quest. Yet at the tail end of a long life, he's in the metaphysical accounting room wondering if he'll come up far shorter than he imagined possible.

What makes Qoheleth unusual is that he shares his midnight anxiety with us—and in the Bible, no less! We're accustomed to turning to religion for absolutes and assurances, guidelines to safeguard us from precisely the sort of self-doubt plaguing Qoheleth. We don't want to come to the end of rigorous years to wonder if we missed the boat and squandered our "one wild and precious life," in poet Mary Oliver's phrase. Qoheleth offers his experience as a flashing neon warning for the rest of us. Turn, turn, turn, indeed!

Some readers find in Qoheleth's questioning a weakness in faith that skates the perimeters of atheism and undermines the God-fearing. Early rabbis agreed, arguing that Ecclesiastes didn't belong among the sacred writings, since reading it "did not make the hands clean." Qoheleth's is a testimony soiled by the inconvenient truths of real life. But he never claims to be a prophet or rabbi. Rather, Qoheleth is a thinker and seeker. As such, he's one of the most modern characters to be found in the Old Testament. Like many at home in our pews today—and others who've relinquished their seats as well—Qoheleth is a "searching believer." He's not content to squat comfortably on tradition like a hen on an egg. He must crack the egg and examine its contents, demanding that received dogma jibe with his lived experience. He won't accept hearsay religion. And he's not going to pretend for you, either. For that, some of us might be grateful.

## How to read Ecclesiastes

This much is true: some of what passes for religious commitment in this world is lacey pious veneer over vanity and emptiness. If we want to go deeper, and to mean what we say in our creeds, we may have to be a shade more honest with God and ourselves—an undertaking both difficult and dangerous. We have to make a clear-eyed tally of our genuine, comprehensive net worth, as Qoheleth does, hopefully at an earlier stage of life than he did. This volume of the Scripture Classics series will be especially helpful for those who identify as searching believers: devoted but not self-deceived, lovers of God who are likewise lovers of truth even when inconvenient. Ecclesiastes 3 bears a message not just for faithful churchgoers but also for those who view themselves as "the loyal opposition": perched in the pew by the door, perhaps, or already seeking answers elsewhere. Qoheleth is the patron saint of adolescents who won't go to Mass anymore without a better reason than the ones they've heard so far. Qoheleth is a friend to the person unwelcome in the communion line because of personal experience that doesn't match delivered teaching. Qoheleth is in conversation with young adults pretty convinced that reality is more complicated than what traditional religious answers acknowledge. Reading Qoheleth affirms those who feel burned by institutions whose authority has been mishandled. For the searching believer, and for the Qoheleth in all of us, a surprising biblical companion emerges to wade with us through the mess and muddle that is life.

# ONE

# Who's in Charge?

FOR EVERYTHING THERE IS A SEASON,
AND A TIME FOR EVERY MATTER UNDER HEAVEN.

T ime is the stuff of which our days are made. While we have time, every possibility under heaven remains true for us. When we run out of time, it's as if the stars fall from the sky and the world ends. Since time is crucial to our being, it's important to come to terms with it. What does it mean to say there's time enough for everything? Is it good news—or the worst possible news—that everything has its season?

When I was growing up, my mother watched the soap opera *Days of Our Lives.* At the start of each episode, one of the better known actors, Macdonald Carey, intoned a solemn voice-over: "Like sands through the hourglass, so are the days of our lives." By the standards of daytime television, that declaration seemed ponderous. There goes time, slipping through our fingers despite all attempts to hang onto a grain of it.

The thesis of Ecclesiastes may well be contained in a one-line voice-over written for daytime TV. This is Qoheleth's piercing cry: Time rushes by, and all it holds is vanity! His word for vanity, repeated thirty-eight times across the book, is more akin to vapor or breeze. Time is a breeze that murmurs gently through our rooms, rustling the curtains as it passes in one window and out another. We enjoy its caress even as it moves beyond us, and nothing we can do will hold it back.

This is a confounding situation for us mortals bound to time's non-negotiability. It's why we often hear this poem in Ecclesiastes as a soothing counterpoint to our anxiety about time. There's time enough for everything, we console ourselves. All is in its proper place and finds its due season.

Regrettably, that's not what the passage says. The implication is that everything happens when its time arrives: hinting at an unseen calendar that we can only guess at. It doesn't describe an abundance of time, or promise its trustworthiness. Only that the control of time's flow isn't in our hands.

What's more, there's going to be time for everything—not just what we want but all the things we surely don't want. Ecclesiastes 3 is a seven-couplet poem about life's polarities, *all* of which will have their season, like it or not. Its logic rests on the creation story of Genesis in which day follows night, dry land balances water, and female complements male. Once sin enters the world, the final polarity snaps into place as evil counters good. The poem in Ecclesiastes describes the consequences of those dual realities.

While we seek comfort for our anxiety regarding the jagged aspects of time, the polarities logged in this poem are morally neutral statements. Time makes room for fourteen pairs of elements, twenty-eight items altogether. In Hebrew numerology, multiples of seven are shorthand for totality. We're given to understand that time will contain every-thing—a statement of fact, not a consolation.

## SURFING THE POLARITIES

We consider this first couplet with eyes wide open and the pitiless facts on the table. Time isn't a basket for everything we hope to collect. And there are no guarantees time will progress in orderly fashion with all unfolding as it should. Every-thing will have its time: from birth and death to war and peace. We are forewarned.

A short session of primal screaming is not out of order here. Most of us would prefer a little more control over what happens in time. We'd like our days to resemble the organized dream closets we see in catalogs, with neat cubbies and dividers containing the chaos and making sense of everything inside. Life, Qoheleth assures us, won't be like that. Stay tuned for the wonderful and the terrible, despite your best efforts to engage one side of experience only and to fortify yourself against the possibility of the other.

My friend Mike did everything humanly possible to have a benign experience of life. You won't meet a humbler, kinder man, one more sincere and hardworking. Yet Mike's years in the seminary did not end with ordination. His later marriage to a woman he adored ended sadly in divorce. Mike hoped next to be the best possible father to his daughter. But Lucy was a girl determined not to be parented.

By the time she reached her teens, Lucy seemed hell-bent on self-destruction. She ran with the wrong crowd and had epic shouting matches with both parents. Mike dreaded what else Lucy was doing that he didn't know about. What scared him most, as it does most parents of ungovernable daughters, was that Lucy might become pregnant and drop out of school. This was the worst-case scenario, the one devil under heaven her father hoped to spare her. Mike spent every waking hour trying to think of a way to rescue his poor child from a deepening downward spiral toward chaos.

Mike is such a mild and courteous man that I knew he was desperate when he admitted that, short of breaking a chair over his daughter, he didn't know how to stop her from doing what she

14

was determined to do. The worst-case scenario arrived like sands through the hourglass: Lucy showed up at home pregnant and miserable. Her father's nightmare had materialized. All that was left to Mike was his response.

There are many ways a bad situation can get worse. Some parents will scream and yell and blame. Some throw the girl out of the house and say: *It's your mess. Deal with it.* Others—even Catholic parents I've known, to be honest—drive their teenager straight to an abortion clinic. But Mike says an angel took his hand and held his tongue. First he cried with Lucy at her news. Then he agreed to support her through this crisis. That decision provided his daughter with the needed security to stay at home and finish high school. As months passed, Mike observed with amazement how this greatly feared pregnancy and birth changed his daughter—for the better. Lucy was transformed from an uncontrollable terror of a girl into a caring and responsible mother. When the worst possible thing Mike could imagine actually happened to his daughter, it turned out to be the hour of her salvation.

Years later, Lucy herself admits that the birth of her beautiful daughter saved her life. The crowd she'd traveled with was rough and dangerous. Her life had become a car with no brakes, and she'd already covered her eyes expecting the crash. A teenage pregnancy could have been that fatal collision. It might have set her on a relentless spiral of poverty, lost chances, and despair. Her father's decision to love and not to punish was crucial. It provided Lucy with the brakes to slow down, consider her course, and choose another direction.

Can a teen pregnancy (which is, on the spectrum of life's polarities, a bad thing) provide a salvific outcome (a good thing)? Our Christmas story doesn't disprove this notion. It certainly changed Lucy, Mike, and everyone affected by their story. Lucy was rescued from her fatal attractions. Mike got to be the best possible father for his daughter—through the worst-case scenario of his dreams for her. When parents express anxiety about the choices their teenagers are making, I now invite them to concentrate less on what their kids might do—since no one has yet devised a way to force a burgeoning adult—and more on what they as parents will do, no matter what their offspring might choose.

## LOSING CONTROL

We don't control the pendulum swings of reality. We're not in control of more than ourselves—and often, not even that. Loss of control is generally viewed as a bad thing. Certainly it can be. Outside of an amusement park ride or a skydiving lesson, freefall experiences are often negative. I want to be in charge of my life. I want to be the governor of my time and decision making, my finances and property, my emotions and relationships. If I'm honest, I admit I want things to go my way as much as possible. Having my agenda met is basically what I mean by having life under control.

How much time do I actually have this type of control? It breaks down with alarming frequency. I want to maintain my weight. Then I cross paths with an open bag of potato chips. I mean to be the very soul of kindness—until a neighbor's ceaselessly barking dog ignites the violence in my heart. I plan on accomplishing chores, only to engage a painful shoulder that curbs my ability to do much of anything. Projects and deadlines loom on the calendar. Then an old friend drops into town and scatters my productivity to the winds.

And these are tiny slips of the hand at the controls. Bad news, loss of employment, sickness, tragedy, or grieving a death can derail years of our lives and often does. We're as influenced by what happens during seasons of no control as we are the product of our choices and intentions.

Jesuit spiritual director Bernie Owens notes that God works with what IS. The Potter works the clay in hand, not some ideal of the clay. If time includes everything possible along its spectrum, then whatever arrives is something God can use and needn't go to waste. We may choose to discard some experiences as worthless, unacceptable, unredeemable. But surrendering precisely such events to God's purposes might be a more valuable decision.

Christian faith, after all, requires us to do the same with our most despicable deeds and darkest passions: to give our "sins," by any other name, to God. It's a terrifying thought, since religious training teaches us to present the exact opposite: only our most shiny prayers and virtuous acts. We dread that God might guess, much less lay claim to, our other, deplorable side. Yet the theology of forgiveness, central to our faith, insists we bring our sins forward. The Potter wants the deformed clay back, to make something useful from it, that nothing may be wasted.

The cross staked at the center of our religion pins the polarities of human experience together, birth and death, violence and peace, so that even the worst elements of our history can be redeemed. The longer we withhold the stinking rotten parts and bring only the best face to church, the longer the world remains in tatters.

It can still be unsettling that God wants our garbage more than our piety. Anne Lamott, author of *Plan B: Further Thoughts on Faith*, admits to being shaken when her pastor preached that Jesus loves the worst person in history so much that he would have died just for him. Anne declares, "This drives me crazy, that God seems to have no taste, and no standards. Yet on most days, this is what gives some of us hope."

If there's hope for us where we are, trapped inside the hourglass, it's this. Everything can happen, and will happen—and everything can also be redeemed. Time is a problem you and I can't solve. We have to live with it, trusting that God is the Lord of history and that God holds the solution to every problem in time.

*Eternal God, we live under the shadow of time and its uncertainty. We hope for happiness and dread the approach of suffering. Give us grace, moment by moment, to be the person we desire to be, especially in the hour we fear most. Drive us to seek forgiveness for the harm we do so that your will may be done, on earth as in heaven. Amen.*

# TWO

# You Are Here

A TIME TO BE BORN, AND A TIME TO DIE;
A TIME TO PLANT, AND A TIME TO PLUCK
UP WHAT IS PLANTED.

lderly Catholics recall an era of church
deeply devotional in character. Into her
nineties, my friend Mary maintained a
strong allegiance to the Sacred Heart of Jesus
and the Immaculate Heart of Mary. These im-
ages hung on the walls of her home, where she
lived with her husband and raised their two boys.
When their sons were grown, Mary and her husband moved to a small apartment, and the two
Hearts went with them. Finally, Mary's husband
died. Since she couldn't live alone anymore, Mary

entered a care facility. The Hearts went with her.

Gradually, Mary's memory faded. She didn't always know her sons when they came to visit. Eventually, Mary didn't get out of bed much. On a warm Friday night in June, she let go of her life on earth. When her sons came to gather up her tiny pile of belongings, they found the two framed Hearts. And they realized their mother had died on the night of the Feast of the Sacred Heart of Jesus—just hours before the start of its twin feast on Saturday, the Immaculate Heart of Mary. Their mother had died between the two Hearts she'd loved most. Did she, whose own past had become unfamiliar to her, sense what day it was? Is there such a thing as a time to die, and did Mary choose hers—or was it chosen for her?

Time is mysterious. And timing, even more so. Things happen. Are they part of a plan? Sheer coincidence? Willed and chosen and brought into being? Two definitive words bracket the human experience: birth and death. Most of us would not claim to make either choice for ourselves. Whatever happens in between—all the planting and plucking, as Qoheleth would say—is our jurisdiction. But that such authority ever comes to us at all, and the hour that we lose it, is not up to us.

How brilliant to hold together the four elements of existence in a small couplet! All that we can't control, and all that we can, are measured out so simply. These elements—birth and death, planting and plucking—are the tent pegs staking out the territory of our humanity. They are our four directions—our wind and water, earth and sky.

Pope Paul VI delivered a passionate declaration about this solemn reality: "Somebody should tell us, right at the start of our lives, that we are dying. Then we might live life to the limit, every minute of every day. Do it! I say. Whatever you want to do, do it now! There are only so many tomorrows." The urgency of sands trickling through the hourglass compels us to act and not delay. If you find yourself anywhere along the spectrum between birth and death, no matter how near or far to those definitive poles, it's time to be planting and plucking.

What can we plant today? What needs harvesting?

Some of us may feel uncertain where to start. Qoheleth insists the time for beginning is behind us. None of us stands on the brink of deciding whether or when to dive into life. We're plunged in already. Mall maps testify with red-dot clarity: *You Are Here.* But where do we *go* from here?

Helpfully, Pope Paul VI had more words of advice: "Everyone who got where he is had to begin where he was." The good news is our present placement will serve admirably. Whatever circumstances, relationships, and contexts surround us, they're worthy tools for the trek toward our future selves.

Is there a spiritual compass to direct us there? How about this: "The spiritual life is first of all a life. It is not merely something to be known and studied, it is to be lived." Thomas Merton wrote these words in *Thoughts in Solitude,* and he sounds just a tad impatient with folks who want to pray and study their way to a more spiritual existence. We're obliged to live, Merton suggests—not saddle up to ride off to a pious otherworld where our daily activities are beside the point. That leaves us standing in the field again with planting and plucking to be done, that red dot hovering over our heads: You are here. Which is the best and only place from which to move forward.

## First the planting

If we're fortunate enough to have a garden or a flowerbox, we may do all right with petunias. But planting is more complicated when it comes to the soil that is ourselves. Nonetheless, we're fairly certain when others do it badly. A story is told about a man we'd agree planted a noxious garden: King Herod. When that infamous biblical king was dying, he knew how little love there was for him among his subjects. Here was a man who'd lived intimately with his crimes. Herod had banished one wife and child to marry another, later putting his second wife and several sons to death. Herod was a notorious killer of rabbis who got in the way, and, according to Matthew's witness, he commanded a slaughter of babies in hopes of securing his throne. So when his own death was imminent, Herod ordered that one man in every noble household be executed the same hour the king expired. That way, Herod reasoned, if no one wept for him at his death, at least there would be weeping.

Say what you will about Herod's values, but the man was dedicated to his method! Herod lived and died by the sword, his planting and plucking being entirely consistent. If we learn anything from reviewing the gardens of those who sow greed, ambition, and violence, it's that consistency isn't always a virtue. We can be dead straight in our direction and dead wrong about it too. Life's polarities require constant reassessments and adjustments. Some situations call for infinite gentleness. Others require a firm hand. Both can be ways of planting something new or harvesting something ready. If we're unyielding in our method, a lack of yield may be what we retrieve. Remember the gospel story of the carefree, crazy sower? He scatters seed on ground both receptive and rocky, in the field and on the footpath. His methodology seems blind and wasteful. He seems to put more faith in the vitality of the seed than in the quality of the earth. The sower isn't careless. His wanton generosity is love personified.

Take an inventory of what you're planting these

days. Is it anxiety about world affairs, fanned into panic each time you watch the news? Suspicion about categories of others who seem strange, even dangerous? Frustration with your boss, your job, your attempts to locate meaningful work? Irritation with a spouse who doesn't listen, who talks too much, who is ominously silent? Regret for mistakes of the past? Fantasies about a future you take no steps to bring into being? We plant thoughts and attitudes, habits and decisions every hour of the day. Much of that time we may be careless sowers, scattering seed we haven't identified and which may spread invasive, malignant vines that choke the life out of everything else in our garden.

Now envision what you hope to produce with your life harvest: Happiness? Warm family relationships? Peace of mind? Purposeful service? A compassionate heart? A holy example? Try to be as specific as you can about what you hope to achieve while the sands of the hourglass are still sprinkling down. If we don't choose deliberately who we intend to be, we may be surprised at who we become.

Planting turns out to be not so mysterious a task after all. Choose, know, and trust the seed you're using. Sow once; tend daily. If you want peace, reinforce each peaceful impulse and pluck up weeds of contention. Fashion the soul you want to live with. If you don't like the way your life feels on the inside, it's your privilege and responsibility to change that.

## THEN THE HARVEST

The hikers' creed says the journey is the destination. This mirrors Saint Paul's injunction to the Galatians that whatever we sow, we will surely reap. Catherine of Siena said, "All the way to heaven is heaven." To which Richard Rohr often adds, "And it's hell all the way to hell." Endings and beginnings are related. I can't sow death and expect to harvest life. I can't harbor hatred in my heart and be a loving person.

My favorite way to view this thesis comes from farmer-novelist Wendell Berry. He says it's no use dreaming your whole life of being a ballet dancer if you spend your days as a pig farmer. In the end, Berry cautions, pigs will be your style.

Don't want to be a pig farmer? Stop raising pigs. Planting rutabaga is no way to harvest watermelon. These are obvious rules, yet we're often startled to discover that harboring prejudice turns us into bigots. If we inwardly criticize each person we meet, we become judgmental. I spent decades paralyzed by the fear of taking risks before I realized the only way to rid myself of that sick feeling in my stomach was to become a risk taker and develop courage. What we hope to be someday we have to start being today.

Be bold in imagining the person you hope to harvest in the long run. Why aim at being nice or harmless when you can be a hero or a saint? That may sound like an impossible goal from where you currently stand under the red dot. But it's not impossible for God. A Yiddish proverb says, "God is an earthquake, not an uncle." We tend to leave God out of the equation in assembling a life plan, as if everything depends on us. We mentally sequester the divine in the church zone or the morality zone, where we don't have to encounter God until we're in need or on our best behavior. But God won't be confined like an elderly housebound relative who hopes we visit on Sunday. God is infinite like love and rumbles under our feet everywhere we go. Ever try to outrun an earthquake? You can't. The very ground under your feet is where the powerful energy trembles. The authority of an earthquake is to shake everything up from the foundation. God the earthquake can rattle us from the ground up and transform a great sinner into a grand saint. In fact, it's the only proven method of producing saints.

It's heaven all the way to heaven, Catherine says. Or hell all the way to hell. Each day's small harvest resembles the final one. Not happy with the yield lately? The time to make changes is now.

This reminds me of my friend Beryl, in whose company I always feel welcome and cherished. It's not just me who feels so valued: it's also every other friend in her orbit, as well as the waitstaff in the restaurant, the store clerk, and the stranger on the street. Everyone gets the Beryl treatment. Being around Beryl is so wonderful I secretly want to move into the apartment next door and bask in her sunshine forever. One day it occurred to me that it must be more wonderful still to *be*

Beryl. Why spend my life simply being the recipient of such welcome when I can become a conduit of love like her? My friends will tell you I am light-years from being such a cosmic lover at this time. But the only way to get there is to go there.

### A TIME TO DIE

Death never sounds right or real to us. And why should it? We're made for life. Taking one breath after another is all we know how to do. Death isn't something we ever get used to. It can never be as natural to us as breathing.

Since life is our native territory, death comes to us like a stranger. Yet in his "Canticle of the Sun," Francis of Assisi embraces Death as our Sister. He understands she's not really a stranger but has always been close by, in our house. Mostly she's silent. But when she speaks, everyone listens. Which supplies another corollary to Catherine of Siena's proposition: all the way to life is life, and all the way to death is death. You and I may feel like death is a stranger, yet we're invited to die to something every day: Our opinions. Our will. Our desires. We may not know Death with a capital D, but we're well acquainted with dying long before we arrive at the final hour.

One thing's for sure. Those who haven't practiced self-denial and have insisted on their will being done in every hour will wrestle with Death as with a sworn enemy. Her No will feel like poison to the ego—and it is. Folks who have learned to say no to themselves along the way can embrace Death as a sister when she arrives to whisper the gentle ultimate No—which, by then, may sound as sweet as Yes.

*Source of all life, we don't express our thanks enough for the totality of life— for sight and sound, color and variety, love and friendship and solitude. We thank you for the opportunity of each hour, for the freedom to choose, to turn and turn again. Focus our attention on the beauty and possibility inherent in each moment. May we live with courage and die with grateful hearts. Amen.*

# THREE

# Not All the News Is Good

A TIME TO KILL, AND A TIME TO HEAL;
A TIME TO BREAK DOWN, AND A TIME TO BUILD UP.

E ach Sunday morning, my favorite altar server performs a minor miracle. She walks from the back of the church to the front, carrying high above her head the processional cross on its long wooden pole. This skinny little girl is only a third as tall as the pole she bears so confidently at the head of the procession. She's really just a kid with tiny silver ballet flats peeping out from under her white acolyte robe. Yet her smile lights up the church as she leads the liturgical ministers and presider forward. This kid loves her job.

One particular Sunday, an infant baptism added some extra drama to the Mass. The happy family held the baby in the sanctuary at the baptismal font, as our pastor performed the sacrament. My favorite acolyte stood by, her processional cross resolutely lifted over the scene. Meanwhile, excited relatives snapped photos around the group. One enormous young man who could have been a linebacker lunged forward with his Nikon to take a shot. This hulk of humanity didn't notice the impact when he whacked the acolyte soundly with his elbow in passing. The girl swayed one way, the cross on the pole teetered the other. It looked like an impossible save. Yet somehow that plucky girl righted herself, kept the pole aloft, never hit the carpet. Straightening her shoulders, she beamed at the assembly to announce her pleasure at the silent victory. Her grin told it all: This cross will not be dishonored. Not on my watch!

I think of that smiling kid in the silver ballet flats sometimes when I'm in danger of losing my balance, when the week's events find me careening out of control. Life can be a grand opportunity—and a terrible problem. Just when I've got it together, something manages to come loose. Is this my fault, or is it that "other guy" who always seems to come out of nowhere to body-slam my precarious efforts? Jesuit retreat master Joseph Tetlow outlines the predicament succinctly: "The problem is that I am from a dysfunctional family, work in a dysfunctional job, and am surrounded by neurotics, with whom I fit perfectly." So the problem *is* that other guy. And the problem is me.

In other words, human existence is a botched proposition from the roots up, and chaos will have its hour. This shouldn't surprise us. Just look around. Or better yet, look within: every impulse for good or ill lives in embryo in our hearts. It's not like we haven't had fair warning. The Genesis creation story provides the blueprint for human failure: God creates the world from original chaos and sets it in balance. Free choosers enter the picture, freely choosing self-will over divine will. In doing so, we opt for chaos. Adam and Eve don't take the fall for this alone. If I carried a clicker around recording how often I choose my will over "thy will" in a given day, I'd be afraid to see the tally. Saint Paul seems to have taken such an inventory. He admits in his Letter to the Romans: The good I wish I did, I don't do. And the bad I wish I didn't, I grab onto with both hands. Tetlow's assessment of our plight resonates here. Paul does have a dysfunctional job (apostle to the uninvested) and is surrounded by neurotics (read his letters again, or Acts of the Apostles, if you have doubts). We can presume the family in Tarsus that produced this strictest of Pharisees fit the dysfunctional profile as well as yours or mine. I can guarantee mine!

Luke explores the flawed blueprint further through the character of the devil who slips in and out of his gospel story. The devil first appears to Jesus in the desert at the time of his great test. Three times Jesus mightily chooses God's will over his own. Foiled, the devil doesn't quit right there in chapter 4. He simply departs "until an opportune time." That time comes on the Mount of Olives in chapter 22. Jesus confronts the mob come to arrest him and declares, "This is your hour, and the power of darkness!" The opportune time may wear a sea of new faces, but it's the same old chaos: self-will over divine will.

Chaos never goes away completely. Destructive forces remain at work in a world that's been dying since the birth of our sun. There will always be more time for killing, more time for things to break down. Chaos seeks its opportune time, and while it may be thwarted here and there, it will have its season. The devil, as Luke says, will always be back for more.

## KILLING VS. HEALING

Killing crouches at one end of the line in this poem, with healing dangling at the other. Are we to view these two forces as somehow held in a moral balance? They don't sound morally aligned to us. Killing seems really bad, and healing really good. Is it possible under any conditions to say: "Today it is right and just to kill"? Will there be time enough tomorrow for healing and saving? Sphinx-like, Qoheleth makes no judgment about these terms but merely acknowledges both forces as realities within history. Sometimes there is killing. Sometimes there are heroic attempts to save life. This is the world we live in.

We may hear this couplet in the poem as

37

fraught with political implications. It helps to note that no one in the third century BC was rolling out Just War Theory. All wars seemed like holy wars to the people of Israel, convinced it was the Lord who led them into battle, choosing victors and vanquished in advance. A debate on capital punishment likewise would have sounded ludicrous to a community with established guidelines in the Mosaic law about when it was good and proper to kill someone. According to that law, God required some killing as an obligation and duty. What's most disturbing in the historical books of the Old Testament is that wholesale episodes of slaughter are taken for granted, if not presented as part of the divine plan for Israel.

Of course, we have to be entirely honest and acknowledge that the most violent death at the center of the New Testament is frequently presented in Christian theology as something God pre-ordains, plans, and requires. Our loving God prophetically plots the death of the Son to achieve a higher purpose, and is "pleased" to crush the Beloved in infirmity. Does this mean the crucifixion of Jesus is history's ultimate "time for killing"?

This reminds me of a seminary professor who introduced himself to a new class as a moral theologian. One of the seminarians replied: "Well, I should hope so! Are there any *immoral* ones?" When some Christians talk about God's saving plan being fulfilled by nailing the Son to the cross, it can sound like a decidedly immoral theology. As Jesus says, even we who are wicked know how to do good for our children! We might produce a kinder, gentler roadmap to salvation. The loving God who creates the universe and forgives sin with boundless compassion doesn't seem compatible with a bloodthirsty deity who desires and plots the murder of Jesus through centuries of painstaking prophecies. Even if this is good medicine, we're not sure we can trust this kind of doctor.

To gain admittance to the mystery of the cross, we might seek passage through the door of love rather than ritual killing. It's important to take a step away from ancient practices of blood sacrifice, where the death of a lamb or bull is the focal point of the event. Divine love is the focus of the "Christ event": love propels the incarnation of

Jesus, the years of his ministry, the surrender at the cross, and the victory of Easter. This gracious, spacious, boundless love is what God chooses—not the most brutal death on record. But because it's the nature of love to be willing to suffer for the sake of love, when the time for suffering arrives, the surrender must come.

What's most startling about this "time for killing" is that it becomes the ultimate "time for healing" in the story of humanity. When humans choose to kill, the best we achieve is self-satisfaction. Such killing may express inner violence or sheer malice. It may halt the advance of an enemy, quench a desire for vengeance, or adhere to some numbed justice that seeks to cancel one death with another. Human killing can never bestow healing, because hatred is not a medicine. Love alone can bind the wounds of history. Love is the only power that ever has.

### THE BREAKDOWN AND THE BUILDUP

In his frank and insightful book *What Is the Point of Being a Christian?* Dominican Father Timothy Radcliffe recounts a story about a famous rabbi who receives a letter from a man in deep distress. "I would like your help," the man wrote. "I wake up each day sad and apprehensive. I can't concentrate. I find it hard to pray. I keep the commandments. But I find no spiritual satisfaction. I go to the synagogue, but I feel alone. I begin to wonder what life is about. I need help." The rabbi returns the letter to the man, underlining the most prominent word in each sentence: *I, I, I, I.*

"I" am always a problem: to myself but also and often to others. The ego self is the opposite of the loving self—and opposition appears to be its campaign. The most innocuous "I" statements contain a tinge of the adversarial: there has to be a "you" on the other side of the table over whom the "I" seeks to assert itself. The cure for the endless battle between "you" and "I" is finding the way to "we." This is the path of love and the only way to true happiness. The necessity of "we" is discovered as early as Genesis: it's no good for the solitary person to remain alone. Yet multiplying people doesn't solve the problem. If I persist in blaming "you"—as Adam and Eve do—there's no "we," just a couple of "I"s bucking heads. Two brothers don't necessarily make a "we" either, as the story of Cain and Abel proves. When one sibling envies another, you can wind up with a corpse and a murderer.

Plenty of marriages are composed of two "I"s in fierce competition for control of the agenda. And Abel is hardly the only fratricide on record: in some families, everyone claims to be the corpse! How do we break down the insidious "I" factor that keeps us apart? How do we encourage the spirit of shared life and purpose? The table at the center of our worship holds the secret. Eucharist is about shared life: you and I, God and us. As Pope Francis says, "The Eucharist is the sacrament which brings us out from individualism." It's almost senseless to claim that "I" go to Mass: we gather together! When a person uses that well-worn phrase, "I don't get anything out of Mass," the most obvious difficulty is that someone is attempting the unlikely: to have a solitary experience in the midst of a party. We the church are a eucharistic people. I'm pretty sure there's no such thing as a eucharistic person.

We may not get it the first time—or the thousandth time—we approach that table. We come back until we realize that we're one with the altar server in the silver ballet flats, and the excited fellow with the camera, and the happy family with the baby, and everyone else in the church in varying states of comprehension or mystification. Once we gain an appreciation of our unity, of course, we just come back for the party.

*God of mystery and majesty, you are the love at the center of all things. You are the surrender of the cross, and the food on the table. You break down our loneliness and are the source of our deep unity. Defend us in the hour of evil, and fill us with a longing for your good will. Amen.*

# FOUR

# *Keep Your Boots on the Ground*

A TIME TO WEEP, AND A TIME TO LAUGH;
A TIME TO MOURN, AND A TIME TO DANCE.

Young people can't imagine being old. That's just as well. Once I mentioned to a teenage niece in a casual conversation that I wake up with some pain every day. That tenderhearted girl burst into tears for my sake. In her experience, pain is something that goes away in a little while. Pain isn't supposed to be a permanent fixture, part of the package deal of living. That her aunt has pain that will never go away sounded like a tragedy to her. I had to stifle a smile as I tried to reassure my niece that pain becomes less of a big deal the longer you live, the more of it you experience. Somehow that didn't come out as comforting as I intended it to be.

Pain is a shock to infants, who scream bloody murder until the least discomfort ends. Everyone over forty, though, adjusts to a minor degree of suffering on a regular basis. Something always hurts—head, heart, muscles, joints—and depending on who you are, maybe lots of things hurt fairly often. Most of us learn to cope with distress of many varieties. My shoulders may get sore from hours of typing, but I have to earn a living. Your knees may ache from arthritis, but you're not going to give up walking. Our hearts may be devastated from relationships gone awry, but we still have to make supper. That's just the way it is. *It* being the human condition.

It's been said: "If you can say YES to pain, there is no pain." I'm not convinced this is true, or how it's meant to be true. So far it's not been true for me, but maybe I'm not saying *yes* loudly enough. For the record, saying no to pain isn't much help either. Maybe conversations with the body are a waste of breath—although Francis of Assisi did talk to his body, nicknamed Brother Ass, when the going got especially tough. Exercise eases some aches, as does acupuncture and ibuprofen—and a bowl of ice cream can be the best elixir when all else fails. When my friend Dale was dying of brain cancer, he was given morphine every day. He was understandably grim about taking it, so at the second dose I offered to give it to him with ice cream. Despite the fact he was dying, and soon, the promise of ice cream awakened the boy in this sixty-four-year-old man, and he exclaimed, "Why didn't you say so the last time?" After that, Dale grinned each time I presented the drug along with the dulce de leche.

For some kinds of pain, nothing alleviates the anguish. Heartache is like that. It re-pierces the breast with every fresh remembrance. With heartbreak, we keep hurting till the healing settles in. That can take a long time.

Pain becomes depressing when it goes on and on. You get tired of it, like a guest that won't leave, tired of having the same old argument. During three years of physical therapy for two rotator cuff injuries, I felt a decreasing ability to endure the pain the longer I carried it in my body—even as it was receding and I was clearly recovering. When the injury was new and the pain sharp, I had more courage and resolve to recover. As the months of fighting pain dragged on, I broke into tears more often, though there was honestly less pain in each movement. Maybe this explains the "say-YES-to-pain" maxim. Fighting the hurt, or denying it, doesn't make it better and can make it worse. Best to move with it and, if necessary, move on with it. This is what most of us do—especially when we're offered no good alternatives.

## WEEPING AND MOURNING

My Catholic upbringing featured many stories about martyrs tortured for hours or days. Maybe too many movies have gloried in depicting the anguish of Jesus on the cross: that long afternoon steeped in suffering that defies our ability to grasp it, however long we gaze at a crucifix. How do you do that? Doesn't the deeply tormented person have to find a way outside of the agony, or above it, before it shatters the mind along with the body? The gospels record seven sayings of Jesus torn from the depths of his affliction and flung into the world like a final Sermon on the Mount of Misery. No gospel claims all seven sayings. Mark and Matthew report only the opening line of Psalm 22: "My God, my God, why have you forsaken me?" Luke and John each report three other sayings but not the same three. Even if Jesus spoke just once, through the pain and struggle of each breath, we wonder: How you do recall a psalm under such conditions, even a single line of it?

When in pain, I forget many things I want to remember. I forget to pray. During the long seasons rehabbing my shoulders I was up half the night, my arms burning with pain. I might have used those empty, lonely hours to pray. Yet I'm ashamed to admit I didn't think of praying at all. I just wanted the pain to stop so I could sleep. Not a single psalm drifted into my consciousness. The Rosary is made for such nights. Many of us know these prayers by heart. Yet my rosary stayed on the nightstand as the reality of pain filled my consciousness to the brim.

To speak seven times from the cross of human suffering is an amazing thing. Even more remarkable is to say seven very significant things about anguish and faith, forgiveness and need and surrender. Many of us curse through pain and find no blessings rising to our lips. When suffering is our medium, it can obscure the message and even abduct it.

Physical suffering, of course, is only part of the spectrum of what makes us weep and mourn. What we carry in our memories, thoughts, and emotions can be as bad or worse. A woman who'd been physically and emotionally abused as a child told me the emotional abuse caused the deepest and most lasting damage. Bruises might heal in a season, but the words echoed in her soul through the years.

Another woman in the community, Rosemary, was a child of abandonment. Her father walked out when she was little, though she never mentioned it. For as long as we've all known her, Rosemary has been a bit of a pill to swallow. She emotionally bludgeons her friends without warning—what we've come to call sniper attacks. A woman this prickly and difficult might be ostracized in any context except parish life. Even so, we've all gone through phrases of avoiding her while healing from a personal blast. And then one of her oldest acquaintances spilled the beans: "Well, you know her father deserted the family." All of a sudden, things snapped into place for the rest of us. We get it now, where the preemptive strikes come from. Rosemary is frightened of being left behind again. Our task is to find ways to assure her of our constancy, so that she can let go of some of her fear.

Few of us communicate lucidly through our pain. We punch when we need to be held. We push people away when we need them close. We fall silent when we need to tell what's going on. Some surprisingly gentle advice comes by way of Plato: "Be kind, for everyone you meet is fighting a hard battle." If each person's secret misery were made visible, we'd probably find a way to love and forgive everyone. So why not presume a mitigating mystery at the heart of anyone who confounds and irritates you, and let go of every trespass?

In *Soul Survivor*, a compelling study of writers who've tried to make sense of suffering, Philip Yancey writes about Dostoevsky's quest to find answers. In the end, the Russian writer acknowledged that the response of Jesus was not a rational fix for the broken world, but total immersion in its anguish. This includes dispensing grace and love to those who deserve it least, against all reason.

## LAUGHING AND DANCING

When we count our blessings, we list the reasons we have to rejoice. We count those who love us, health and security, a roof overhead, kindnesses received and prayers answered. Our catalogue rarely sounds like the Beatitudes: the list Jesus proposes as reasons worthy of celebration.

Passionist theologian Donald Senior defines the Beatitudes as "lessons from the school of suffering." They celebrate the beauty and the power of God—but in terms that leave us pale with worry. This isn't how we'd prefer to be blessed! We're glad to laugh and dance but don't want to endure all that hard living first. Rufus Jones, a Quaker philosopher, describes the paradox of beatitude: "Losses and crosses, pains and burdens, heartaches and bereavements, empty chairs and darkened windows, are the last of all things to be expected in the list of beatitudes. They were then, and still often are, counted as visitation of divine disapproval." Yet Jesus invites us to celebrate the things we're most likely to identify (however erroneously) as God punishing us!

The kingdom paradox as Jesus teaches it is never on display as bluntly as in the Beatitudes. It's one thing to say the first will be last and the last first—reorganizing the Paradise queue, so to speak. Beatitudes go a step further, discovering happiness in places no one goes looking for it. What makes us laugh and dance in the Beatitudes is that the polarizing elements of Qoheleth's couplets blur into middle ground; weeping and laughing, mourning and dancing aren't so far apart after all. What brings them together is God's constancy. God is as close to us in the midst of evil and suffering as in circumstances we count as more obvious blessings.

God is with us, in poverty and lowliness, in hunger and sacrifices for justice. God mourns with us, shows mercy through us, and wages peace with us. It's God's readiness to be immersed in the most difficult chapters of our lives that turns our suffering into beatitude. William Sloane Coffin spoke of this in the eulogy he gave for his son Alex, who died in a car accident at the age of twenty-four. Coffin declared: "Nothing so infuriates me as the incapacity of seemingly intelligent people to get it through their heads that God doesn't go around this world with his fingers on triggers, his fists around knives, his hands on steering wheels....The one thing that should never be said when someone dies is 'It is the will of God.' Never do we know enough to say that. My own consolation lies in knowing that it was not the will of God that Alex die; that when the waves closed over the sinking car, God's heart was the first of all our hearts to break."

In times of anguish we weep and mourn, but we are not abandoned to despair. In times of joy we laugh and dance, knowing that seasons change, sometimes swiftly. But in all hours of life we find ourselves genuinely blessed. As newly sainted John Paul II avowed, "We are the Easter people and Hallelujah is our song."

*Lord of the dance, I've got my dancing
shoes on. Teach me the steps when my
legs are trembling with weariness under
the burden of life's trials. Bear me up
when I have no strength to continue.
Hold me close so that I can hear your
heart breaking when mine is shattered in
pieces. And when the seasons of blessing
really feel like blessing to me and I
am overcome with joy, I'll dance for
you like a child full of gratitude before
the Giver of every good gift. Amen.*

# FIVE

# *Learn to Discern*

A TIME TO THROW AWAY STONES,
AND A TIME TO GATHER STONES TOGETHER;
A TIME TO EMBRACE, AND A TIME
TO REFRAIN FROM EMBRACING.

L ife is a mystery. But not an absurdity. There may be no rational method in the madness that may govern the years, but there is a discernable rhythm. We feel it lapping in the creation story, in which chaos is organized between darkness and light, water and land, birds and fish, male and female. We hear it in Qoheleth's thumping polarities: throw your stones away, and then gather them together; embrace now, and then refrain. We touch this rhythm in the Beatitudes, as our tangible acts of mercy make us eligible for God's mercy, and our peacemaking reveals our resemblance to God as divine children. The rhythm throbs in kingdom paradoxes: The poor are lifted up; the rich bowed down. The virgin becomes a mother; the mother of many languishes. The sinner knows mercy, and the dead rise.

Life is a mystery that's not absurd but has a kingdom logic to it. How can we learn the kingdom's "new math," to appreciate why the wages of sin once added up to unequivocal death, but now yield the possibility of eternal life? The key to the mystery lies in a single word at the heart of the gospel: forgiveness. It's been estimated that two-thirds of what Jesus teaches in parables, sermons, healings, and sayings is about forgiveness. The need to seek forgiveness and let our lives be turned around is primary. Yet we often prefer to keep sin and its wages in our pocket.

A truck driver in the arid lands of southern California told me this story. He was barreling down a road just out of town when he spied a woman standing on a stretch of open desert, visibly melting in the hot sun. She clearly knew nothing of the terrain into which she'd wandered. She had no hat, her face reddening and perspiring. A bright pink pantsuit and low-heeled pumps testified to her unpreparedness for what she'd undertaken. She was standing much too close to a jumping cactus for comfort, and what was worse, she probably didn't know it.

Yet the trucker drove past without stopping, snorting with delight at her predicament. These stupid tourists! Always getting into trouble. Well, he wasn't going to help a fool out of her foolishness. He drove another quarter mile and saw a flash of something uncharacteristically pink caught on the arm of a Joshua tree. It was, he knew from the silly streamers dangling from its straw brim, that ridiculous woman's hat. Perhaps a sudden hot wind had snatched it from her head and led her to take this ill-conceived stroll off the road. Just then, something snagged the trucker's heart as sharply as the tree had impaled the hat. He didn't know why this sensation—was it pity?—clutched at him so profoundly at the sight of those ludicrous dangling ribbons.

That silly person was risking her life for a

straw hat. Understanding broke over the trucker, and with it a strange sorrow twisted in his chest. Without knowing why, he made a U-turn, detached the hat from the tree, and drove back to the spot where the helpless tourist was still encircled by cacti. The man extracted her from danger, then handed her the hat. As tears started from the woman's eyes and she began to speak her thanks in a language he didn't understand, the trucker fled back to his vehicle and roared down the road.

Telling the story, the truck driver choked on the words, and his own eyes filled with tears. He still couldn't explain it: why he went back for the hat, what prompted him to care for the sort of person he routinely despised. There's a spirit available to us that's better than we are, a spirit of righteousness and holiness, compassion and grace. It prompts us toward the good, even when we have no personal motivation to seek it. Call it conscience, or decency, or humanity. Though we can close our minds and shutter our hearts to its influence, this spirit witnesses to what's right and testifies against us when we go another way. The oppositional testimony may feel like shame, regret, a gnawing in the stomach, a twist of pain in the chest. So long as we're susceptible to the promptings of this guiding spirit, we're never lost. But if we routinely ignore the promptings, there may come a time when they are silenced.

### GATHERING STONES AND THROWING THEM AWAY

Spiritual writer Henri Nouwen spent seven months at a Trappist monastery. During that time he had illuminating insights, which he recorded in *The Genesee Diary*. One involved gathering stones from a riverbed to be used to build a chapel. Just the right sort of stones had to be garnered for the project: granite rather than sandstone. Since all the stones were covered with lime, it was often hard to tell them apart. Also, because they were mired in earth, it was difficult to know the size of a stone when you started to pry it loose. Sometimes the small stone you'd found became an enormous boulder impossible to budge. It took the monks of the abbey more than a year to gather enough stones for a chapel.

Finally, tons of granite rocks were assembled awaiting the mason's construction. You can imagine the monks' dismay when the mason insisted he needed more. The mason explained that laying stone isn't the same as brickwork. You can't simply lay one after another since they're not the same shape. When putting two or three stones together, a space is created. The task becomes to fill the space with not just any stone but the right stone.

Gathering stones is a crucial element of building a single chapel or a whole city. Casting away stones describes the work of dismantling a civilization—a task with which ancient conquerors were familiar. Recall the gospel scene when Jesus and the disciples finally reach Jerusalem. The backwater Galileans are awed by the enormous stones used to erect the Temple, surely the grandest building they've seen. Many stones—some of them eighty tons in weight, forty feet long, eight feet wide, three feet high—are in place on the Temple Mount today with no need of mortar to secure them. It's understandable the disciples are impressed. Yet Jesus assures them these stones will be thrown down. A generation later, in 70 AD, the Romans toppled most of the Temple's massive walls. Considering that it took one hundred and twenty hours of labor to produce a single cubit of this cut stone, the horror of the Temple's destruction must have been anguish for any citizen who witnessed it.

What's true about stone is true about all of life's projects. We must choose our materials with care, placing each activity, decision, or relationship in its proper place and making sure it's the right shape to fit the space: neither too big nor too small, too jagged or too smooth. It's no good to have lots of stones if we don't have the stone we need, the one that fits the space. We also need to be clear-eyed about the way of earthly things: what we build can easily be dismantled, including marriage and family, financial security and career, reputation, health, and any future plans. It's vital not to possess any idea about ourselves or our lives too dearly. Even the massive Temple of Jerusalem, eighty years under construction, was thrown down in a single siege.

In the construction of our lives, we learn that details matter. There are no throwaway decisions or moral corners safe to cut. We build, knowing others may use this foundation on which to build further. We build, also aware that others may find this structure unhelpful, preferring to clear it away to allow some new design to emerge. I once spoke to a Sister about religious life. At that time some people were saying religious life was an old form that had to pass away so the church could discover a new model for service. Others insisted the traditional forms were the best and only way. When I asked this middle-aged Sister what she thought, she was serene about either vision. Though she'd given forty years to her community and anticipated remaining in that identity until death, it didn't disturb her if God had another path prepared for the future that didn't include communities like hers. I was astounded by her peace. She didn't need to possess the only truth, claim the only vision. If her particular stones came down, it was no hardship so long as the living temple of God's choosing remained.

In a thought-provoking reflection on religious community, *The Fire in These Ashes*, Joan Chittister considers founders and foundresses who began their communities as a direct response to needs within their societies and times. Where poor children, or children of color, or female children went without education, communities emerged to open schools. When the sick were dying without care, communities sprang up to start hospitals. What needs does our modern world present, and what forms of service might best meet them? The stones we need require discernment. What needs to be built is also a serious matter for discernment and investment.

## EMBRACING AND REFRAINING

We're tempted to read the couplets presented by Qoheleth as arbitrary groupings of ideas. What do embraces have to do with stones? Surely these two lines share no more than proximity with each other. Perhaps there's more to the coupling than that. Just as human projects rise and fall, take shape or dissolve, so do human relationships. This can seem a forbidding idea to those who live in parts of the country where stability and continuity is prized. I come from the Northeast, where many folks spend their whole lives in one town and find it odd to do otherwise. My father died at eighty in the same house in which he was born. I know folks in retirement who still hang out with friends they've had since high school. Many of my siblings live close enough together to visit often and to know each other's children well.

But an insular lifestyle isn't always possible, even for those who want it. Economic factors can drive people away from the circle of family and familiarity as industries rise and fall. Two generations before me, such forces drove my grandparents to come to this country. And while much of my generation remains linked geographically, two nieces have already chosen to live briefly overseas. The twenty-first century finds us on a planet that seems smaller, more interconnected. Rapid changes in technology keep economies fluid and employment a revolving door. All of this suggests that the next generation will be on the move a lot more than the last generation was. Just as extended families no longer frequently occupy single homes or live a few porches away, more of us will feel the heart tug of distance between us and those we hold most dear.

The last two years I lived in the same city as my young niece Megan. I tried not to be the clingy aunt; we met only a few times a season. I got to know Megan's friends, to participate in her generation's conversation and to explore their values. It was a rare and wonderful chance to embed with young adults less than half my age, to enjoy their companionship and trust, and I cherished every minute of it. When it came time for Megan to move away to a great opportunity and to be closer to her fiancé, every nerve in my arms wanted to clasp her close, to keep her near. Thank God I was twenty-something too, once. When it's time to fly, love opens its arms wide and lets go.

*Creator of hard stones and soft hearts, you give us the freedom to build whatever we wish: cities, communities, careers, homes, relationships. We remember too that a stone carelessly rejected may be the cornerstone vital to the whole structure. Let your Holy Spirit guide us to discern what needs to remain and what requires change, when to hold on and when to let go. Amen.*

# SIX

# *Travel Lightly*

A TIME TO SEEK, AND A TIME TO LOSE;
A TIME TO KEEP, AND A TIME TO THROW AWAY.

"Things are the thieves of time." So says journalist Nathan Gardels in a gripping documentary, *The 11th Hour.* This thievery is an interesting proposal, since the invention of these same things was supposed to help us *save* time, to make more time for the pursuits we really care about. The industrial revolution shortened the work week and gave us the weekend. Then the technological revolution took back the gains. Now many people are virtually tied to work all the time, on nights and weekends and through vacations. "Things" have picked our pockets and stolen our life away! Should we care, and can we do anything about it?

The computer has changed the world and mostly for the better. It makes most of what we once did by hand so much neater, quicker, and simpler. It provides us with lightning-fast connections that we can hardly imagine living without. Suddenly everyone we ever met and billions more we'll never meet are accessible in a heartbeat. This is a mixed blessing. As Thomas Edison remarked at the invention of the telegraph: "We are in great haste to construct a magnetic telegraph from Maine to Texas; but Maine and Texas, it may be, have nothing important to communicate." Each morning as I delete most of my e-mail unread (and wish I could toss a great deal of the remainder after I've read it), I think of Edison and sigh.

Computers aren't the villains. Nor are video games with their predicable rush of adrenaline, cable television and streaming services that enable our binge-watching, or any number of devices we'd like to finger as the culprits in pickpocketing our time. If things dribble time away from us, if we're distracted and be-plugged, the real culprit is our willingness to be led to the slaughter of our hours. If we want our lives back, our freedom back, if we want to regain our purpose, we have to look at the stones we've been gathering and ask if this is the house we want to live in.

We have to stop making excuses. There's no point in wishing for a deeper, more spiritual experience if we're unwilling to declutter, to make room for stillness and silence—just as we can't long for physical fitness while we persist in sitting on the couch eating Doritos. If we spend every night at the bar, we won't get sober. If we're sick of conflict-ridden family dynamics or the same tired conversations full of foregone conclusions, we can't wait for others to reverse direction and change. Free will makes us the determiners of what becomes of us. If our days are stuffed with things we don't like and don't want, simplification and satisfaction are only a decision away.

The Shakers have taught us "'tis the gift to be simple," but the Quakers are longtime proponents of streamlining life to sharpen one's true purpose and make the best use of time. Thomas Kelly outlines the Quaker ideal of "centering down" in his classic work *A Testament of Devotion.* Centering down involves both a readiness to do and a willingness to renounce—both within easy reach if we're situated in the proper place. Much activity that presently consumes our days will lose its appeal once we gain the center and can view it in perspective. Centering leads to a unification of our fractured, cubicled identities. We have "a whole committee of selves," in Kelly's view: the civic self, the parental self, the financial self, the religious self, the professional self. Religious duty becomes just one more cubicle of obligations vying for our attention, when our life in God could be the natural center from which all else flows.

Prayer is an activity best approached from the center rather than the edge of reality. Yet the edge is where we spend most of our time, orbiting rather than inhabiting what's good and true and essential. When Nouwen spent his months at the Genesee Abbey, he came to see that he was closer to the heart of the world in a place removed from society than he was at the university or giving retreats around the country. In the monastery praying for the world, Nouwen recognized that he "became the world," his soul expanding to embrace all and to bring all to the center with God. "In praying for others," Nouwen reflected, "I lose myself and become the other, only to be found by the divine love which holds the whole of humanity in a compassionate embrace."

Sainthood, a vocation that can seem formidable and complex from the outside, is a matter of great simplicity at its center. To philosopher Søren Kierkegaard, holiness requires only to "will the one thing"—what God wills—in place of the thousand fleeting whims of our own willing. Call it centering down or unity, simplicity or single-heartedness. What we call it matters less than finding a way to ensure that things will not be the thieves of our "one wild and precious life."

### LEMON TREE, VERY PRETTY
Seek the true and the vital. Get rid of what distracts and drains time and purpose. For a long time I held onto items on a wish list of who I was going to be when I finally had the time to become her. One object was a guitar, which I was going to learn to play. Another was a full set of canning

supplies: I meant to resume a hobby of putting up fruits and vegetables. I had a complete volume of Shakespeare's works. I was going to read them this time, not whizzing through as I did back in college. And patches of cloth for when I'd take up quilting, and oil paints for when I'd discover art in me, etc. I hauled these items and more from place to place for that wonderful mythical future day when I become someone else entirely.

Move by move and year by year, I've weaned myself from many of these items, allowing the fantasy of what my life might be to drift away in favor of what it actually is and can be, given the limits of mortality. I don't need a storage unit of dreams to accuse me of what I'm not, or to tempt me from what I need to become. Each decade has revealed how little is necessary to do what's given to me to accomplish. The spirit of decluttering is more prominent in the generations coming up, who prefer not to buy or to own but opt for renting living spaces and time-sharing services. They seem willing to trust more in people than in the false security of things. People under thirty seem to sense, contrary to the consumer culture that bred them, that life is not a grab-fest. Perhaps we've taught them by our sad search for happiness at the mall that the lemon tree is very pretty, but its fruit is impossible to eat.

Eating from the lemon tree in the age of consumerism, we've unearthed the Beatitude wisdom that claims purity of heart is necessary to see God, or even to see clearly. Whenever we hear the word purity, our thoughts attach immediately to sexual matters. But to be pure means to be unmixed, to contain nothing that does not belong. The chastity proper to each state in life is included in that definition but is not the sum of it. Purity is more like centering down or unifying up—bringing everything to the center and to wholeness, and holding it all together with integrity.

Kenneth Boulding, social scientist and Quaker mystic, makes the curious claim that in an era of good intentions and bad information, love without knowledge might destroy us. If this idea sounds backwards, compare it with Martin Luther King Jr.'s declaration: "One day we will learn that the heart can never be totally right if the head is totally wrong." We can't divorce our hearts from our brains, surrendering ethics to the devout and science to the agnostic in a twisted bid to give to Caesar and to God their due territories. To the pure-hearted, all is God's. And while love is an exceedingly powerful force that "never fails" in Paul's estimation, knowledge too exerts real and tremendous authority in this world. When love separates from knowledge, Boulding asserts, the one who loves may have the strength of ten but still doesn't know what to do with it—and that can be terribly dangerous.

During a long wait on jury duty at our courthouse, I conversed with a woman who was overjoyed to meet a fellow Catholic. Although in her sixties, this woman confided she'd never been summoned for jury duty before—which she proudly attributed to the fact that never once in her life had she voted in an election. I was astonished by this claim and asked her why she didn't vote. "I'm a Catholic!" she declared. "I trust in God and the church, not in politics." It was impossible to persuade her that faith might make casting her vote in the public arena particularly significant.

We have only to consider the blind fundamentalism that compels many in political or religious leadership worldwide to see the oppression, prejudice, and violence that's unleashed by those who bury their love in a group identity or an idea— even an idea of God—and reject all further input. This partiality masquerades as "purity," but it's vision out of one eye, lacking depth perception. Holding everything together at the center is not the same as holding favored elements in, and all others at bay.

### SEEK, LOSE, KEEP, TOSS

Karl Rahner proposed that in the future, we will all be mystics or non-believers. The future may already be here. If it takes a mystic to center down, drawing everything together and holding it with integrity and purity of heart, then it's time to embrace our vocation to this kind of vision. Those who don't may claim allegiance to God, creed, or faith community, but their trust remains more in personal impressions and opinions than in the real and the true.

The anonymous writer of *The Cloud of*

*Unknowing* instructed would-be contemplatives of the Middle Ages to focus on three occupations: reading, thinking, and praying. Yet twentieth-century spiritual writer Evelyn Underhill observed that we mostly spend our love conjugating three other verbs: "to Want, to Have, and to Do. Craving, clutching, and fussing." If we want to find something real, we have to lose a lot of our costuming. If we hope to hold onto anything for keeps, we're obliged to throw out a lot of what's temporal: junk possessions, time-dribbling activities, and careless associations. Cleaning out the closet or recycling the contents of the garage can no longer stand in for what it means to simplify our lives. Purification of the heart is ground zero for this task.

*Life at the center of all life, and Love*
*at the center of all love: this is who*
*you are, my God. You know my mind*
*and heart, and you view the clutter*
*accumulated there. Guide me to*

*genuine purity, cleansing my hours*
*of vain pursuits, idle conversations,*
*and wasteful consumption. Lead*
*me to the true and sacred center,*
*where I can discover at last your life*
*in me, which has no end. Amen.*

# SEVEN

# Put Courage on Your Résumé

A TIME TO TEAR, AND A TIME TO SEW;
A TIME TO KEEP SILENCE, AND A TIME TO SPEAK.

Sunday services hold a lot of drama—some of it unintended. One morning at Mass, the usher invited a young couple to bring up the gifts at the time of the offering. The couple had a toddler with them, whom they quickly passed to a grandparent as they left the pew. The child was not happy with this arrangement. He whimpered softly, then loudly declared, "I want my mommy!"

As his parents proceeded up the center aisle

to the altar with the gifts, the child's wailing and tears only became more anguished. "I WANT MY MOMMY!" he cried, over and over. The assembly shuffled and grew uncomfortable, the liturgical moment derailed as no one focused on the gifts being offered, all eyes glued to the struggling, screaming little boy.

Finally, from across the church a little girl raised her voice and broke through the wailing. "You can have MY mommy," she volunteered. Laughter erupted across the church, the moment rescued by a child's spontaneous and sincere generosity. Talk about an offering! This child knew precisely when to speak within a context in which most of us are conditioned to keep silent.

Catherine de Hueck Doherty once prayed: "Lord, give me the heart of a child, and the awesome courage to live it out as an adult." The natural moral courage of children presents itself too many times to be viewed as a fluke. My sister tells about taking her young daughter on a nursing home visit. The sight of the sick elderly, some lucid and many far from it, crowded into colorless rooms in the average care facility can strike fear in the heart of anybody—as if Dickens' Ghost of Christmas Future inhabited such halls, pointing at us with his bony finger. Yet my little niece showed no hesitation. Strolling around the common room, she approached one wheelchair-bound resident after another, complimenting one woman on her pretty pearl necklace, admiring the print pattern on another woman's blouse, asking a third if she needed help with her jigsaw puzzle. Where many would see only illness and decline, maybe even an irrational mortal contagion, this child saw lonely people in need of some cheering up.

Adults in my experience don't always present a flattering contrast. When my friend Dale became hemiplegic, many of his longtime acquaintances stopped coming by, made nervous and uncomfortable by the sight of medical supplies and the smells of the sickroom. One friend, who'd initially volunteered to help with Dale's care, changed his mind because Dale was "too sick" for him to be further involved. If Dale had been less sick, of course, his friend's involvement wouldn't have been necessary. It stunned me at first, then angered me, when I realized how many of Dale's closest friends—churchgoers all—could not or would not cross the threshold of his final illness to meet him in his hour of deep need. In the end, anger gave way to compassion when I recognized how many were plain scared to be around someone who was dying.

Some of us remember when *The Wizard of Oz* was televised annually as a peculiar, off-center Easter special. Maybe this homegrown tale from our heartland *is* an American resurrection story. A scarecrow with straw for a brain is reborn as a philosopher and strategic planner. A tin man with an empty-barrel chest discovers the capacity for love and compassion. A lion afraid of his own tail finds the ability to be brave for the sake of those who depend on him. And, of course, Dorothy and the wizard have to die to their old selves and rise to more heroic natures. They literally rise in a balloon into a higher purpose.

What confused me while watching this show as a child was how the lion ever got into the story. I could appreciate why qualities of the brain and heart, reason and love, were needed to attain wholeness. It was apparent why Dorothy required these two fundamental elements to get her act together back in Kansas. By comparison, courage seemed less significant, more arbitrary. Unlike the other two qualities, courage wasn't visceral: no body part was assigned to this attribute. I wondered why courage got inserted in the essential trinity. Courage seemed a wild hair in an otherwise tightly woven story.

As I get older, I see that the lion belongs and L. Frank Baum got it right. Courage is essential on the journey down this road. If courage needs a body part to fit the triumvirate with brain and heart, I'd give it a hand. If the brain understands and the heart motivates, then courage acts. Great ideas and generous ideals go nowhere if the deed is not actually done.

### TEARING AND SEWING

Here's where church enters the picture. When I ask the middle-schoolers in our parish religious education program what "church" is, they predictably say it's a place you go on Sundays. When I ask why we go there, they grow quiet.

"Why go to church?" I persist.

"To get sacraments," they suggest.

"And why get sacraments?" I ask.

"So that we can completely belong to the church."

"And why is that a good thing?"

"So that we can continue to go to church," they offer.

The circularity of this Christian vision is obvious, even to children, but they can't find a way out of it. They go to church and participate in church rituals in order to belong to church and go to church some more. It sounds like the hollow merry-go-round it is, but they're at a loss to get off or go farther. Church remains this kind of empty identity for many adults who fulfill the Sunday obligation because they're assured it's important—but it's honestly not important to them. Attendance at church is what church means to them; the goings-on in that space don't intersect meaningfully with the rest of life.

We hear a lot about "the Church" while in church—what it teaches, what it offers, what it obliges us to do. This identity of "Church with a capital C" refers to something larger than the building where we pray locally. Often it points to the Magisterium: the teaching authority of Christ passed on to the church from the apostles through ordained leadership. Just as our local experience of church resides in the particular building and community that comprise our parish, so the magisterial aspect of church expresses its universal quality. Still, for the non-ordained, this too is an impersonal idea of church disconnected from where most of us live and breathe and have our being.

The Second Vatican Council offered a new direction from which to approach the idea of church through the wonderfully electric term, "the People of God." Suddenly the vast majority of us could plug in. Instead of "it-church" or "them-church," the People of God delivers "us-church." This identity isn't confined to a building, teaching, or ecclesial office. This sense of church is portable. It goes where we go, enmeshed in and intrinsic to all the concerns we have, the relationships that have meaning for us. If the People of God are also church—not a margin-note definition but a primary one—then the question "Why go to church?" is answered: "To become church, to become conscious of our identity as the People of God, and to carry it into all of our dealings, decisions, and plans."

The root word for church is *ecclesia,* or assembly. The church doesn't house the assembly; the assembly comprises the church. As Evelyn Underhill reminds us: "The church is in the world to save the world. It is a tool of God for that purpose; not a comfortable religious club established in fine historical premises." The church's mission established by Jesus is to go out into the world bearing wonderful news. Jesus had nothing to say about witnessing rituals, attending pious lectures, or holding fundraisers.

When the conversation in church becomes top-heavily concerned with doings in church, it leaves less room for a more vital concern, which is the kingdom of God. This is worrisome. The word *church* comes up only twice in all four gospels, whereas the kingdom is mentioned forty-four times in Matthew's gospel alone. In *Jesus and Judaism,* E. P. Sanders noted wistfully: "Jesus preached the coming of the Kingdom, but it was the Church that arrived." One mustn't be mistaken for the other.

The church is not the kingdom. Yet if the People of God show lion-sized courage, we can be the hand that prepares the way for kingdom's arrival. All aspects of church can work together to create a hopeful, holy space where kingdom can be realized. Now and then we get a glimpse of what this would look like. Twentieth-century Bishop P. Francis Murphy of Baltimore was a tireless advocate of issues people of good will might support: help for the hungry; peace in the world; women's rights in the church; improved interfaith, ecumenical, and race relations. Bishop Murphy didn't embrace single-issue Christianity but rather bought the whole garment. He took seriously the injunction of Jesus against patch-work solutions to intrinsic problems: sewing a new patch on a threadbare cloak never works. Sometimes you have to tear out a panel of the old fabric before you sew in something new. This can be a painful process. All of Qoheleth's polarities involve pain somewhere along their spectrum.

After serving on the National Conference of Catholic Bishops' Committee on Women in the Church and in Society, Bishop Murphy appealed to his brother bishops for a holistic approach. "In our failure to come to grips with the question of patriarchy," Murphy said, "we bishops seem to be buttoning up a coat that has the top button in the wrong buttonhole. No matter how carefully we button the rest of the coat, it will not fit. We cannot adjust by skipping a button. We can't pretend it fits—no matter how nice the coat."

## BE THE LION

Brain and heart are needed to steer and motivate the hand. But the hand must still move to get the work done. Some situations warrant a little mending, while others need more drastic tearing, which can cost us much. We as church can be so much more than the folks who attend rituals on Sunday mornings. We can be the courageous voice that knows when to speak up and advocate for those in need. We can acquire wisdom to know when it's more courageous to remain silent, as Jesus did in the face of his accusers. Careful discernment helps us to distinguish between courageous silence and self-interest.

Jesus repeats the call to lion-hearted living

many times. To the paralytic, he says: "Courage, child, your sins are forgiven." To the woman with the hemorrhage: "Courage, daughter! Your faith has saved you." To the disciples on the stormy sea: "Take courage, it is I; do not be afraid." At the last supper to his friends at table: "In the world you will have trouble, but take courage, I have conquered the world." If the Lord is with us in all these ways— forgiving, rescuing, companioning, conquering— what power can possibly stand against us?

*Almighty and victorious God, we know that if you are with us, no power on earth can persevere against us. We trust in the promise of Jesus to remain with his church all days until the end of the world. With the Holy Spirit as our guide and conscience, steer this community of faith to a bold testimony of what love, forgiveness, and compassion can do. Amen.*

# EIGHT

# Look for the Big Picture

A TIME TO LOVE, AND A TIME TO HATE;
A TIME FOR WAR, AND A TIME FOR PEACE.

Most of us are schooled in binary thinking. As children, we learn the answer to every question is either yes or no, thirsty or not, black or white, up or down. Outcomes involve winning or losing, with very little middle ground sketched out in between. Someone is either a good guy or a bad guy—and once categorized, it's hard to consider any moral ambiguity.

Binary thinking causes a lot of problems. Since we want to win and not lose—and it's either "us" or "them" who's winning—competition becomes more natural to us than cooperation. We tend to join one side of a discussion and demonize the other side. Discussion devolves into debate, and every debate becomes a battlefield. We don't talk; we argue. We don't seek mutual ground in a conflict but simply commence dropping bombs.

Binary thinking is positional thinking. We register for a political party and then bar the doors to admit no ideas from outside our chosen group. We adhere to the traditions of our creed and denounce any other spiritual path as empty, false, or evil. We root for our team, count only the losses of our troops, remain behind the walls of our housing development, and protect the interests of our social class. It's hard to seek nuanced solutions that promote the common good when wearing the blinders of the binary worldview. If life were that simple and reality black and white, binary vision wouldn't be an issue. But rarely is an event or a person entirely pure in character. Times change, and so do people.

Once I met a delightful parish priest from Fiji with a tattoo on the back of his hand. On closer inspection, I recognized it as a skull and crossbones!

Printed underneath this insignia was a single and somewhat startling word, given the man's position in the community: *MAFIA*. I asked the priest if youthful indiscretions had caught up to him when he decided to seek ordination: "I bet you never thought about giving out communion with that hand when you decided to get the tattoo."

He laughed, admitting that at the time he gained the tattoo, he was a teenager. His greatest desire back then had been to join the mafia gang, a name with perhaps more bark than bite. Part of the initiation rite involved tattooing your own hand with the gang name and sign. He remembered it as a painful procedure but worth enduring as the entrance fee to belong to that exclusive group.

And then the priest told me, "You know what the strange thing is? Five members of the original mafia gang went on to become priests. Eight more became policemen. We may have seemed marked for trouble in the beginning, but God earmarked us for other purposes in the end."

If you and I cling to positional thinking, we may observe in the vicinity a gang of teenagers with skull-and-crossbones tattoos and be tempted to call the police. We can't imagine that one day some of them will *be* the police—and the rest of them priests staffing our parishes and giving us moral counsel. If we insist on binary thinking, assigning white hats and black hats to all players, we miss the opportunity to experience the full humanity of those around us. When we withhold from others permission to undergo conversion and surprise us, we curtail our own ability to do the same.

## JESUS LOVES PARADOX

One perspective that shatters binary thinking is paradox. It's a perspective Jesus seems particularly fond of. From the moment a virgin conceives, divinity unites with humanity, and all heaven breaks loose in a deluge of colliding and colluding polarities. The poor babe in the straw is the king of the universe. The carpenter's son is also Son of God. The queue of history reverses as the last become first, the blind see, the lame dance, and the meek inherit the earth. Multitudes are fed on handfuls of bread. Nothing is as it seemed to be. Everything is revealed as more

and less than what we've been told. Sins are forgiven. The dead will rise. All bets are off. Eternity
is now, and God's kingdom arrives in every hour
we say yes to it.

Paradox is both the enemy and the salvation
of binary thinking: it must be both, by definition.
Paradox holds opposing forces in creative ten-
sion, making a third way, or an infinite number
of new ways, possible. This is what Isaiah fore-
told—"See, I am creating new heavens and a new
earth"— and what Revelation confirms: "Behold,
I make all things new." Original sin is at the heart
of the binary illusion. It divided creation—origi-
nally declared an unqualified good—into the polarity of good and evil. The new creation aims to
heal that wound and bring the world to original
integrity again. It does require surrendering all
division in our hearts and our outlook, which we
may be reluctant to give up.

Why does Jesus teach paradox so much?
Because it jars his listeners awake. When rogue
sons are forgiven and celebrated while obedient
sons gnash their teeth outside the party, it's an
upsetting vision. When the shepherd who aban-

dons an entire flock to go after a single wayward animal is dubbed good at his job, we want to protest. Paradox splinters the certainty of the binary behavioral code. It tells us we don't think like God thinks, and it reminds us we can't see as God sees. The paradox of kingdom vision that Jesus outlines prepares us for even more shocking perspectives, as he declares: I am the temple. I am manna from heaven. I am shepherd and gate. I am way, truth, and life. Jesus fuses himself to every portal of divine truth, leaving no space for misunderstanding.

The language of paradox translates, transports, and transcends the way we normally view what's true and leaves us speechless. Kingdom is coming yet already in our midst—how? It's fulfilled in Jesus and also a work in progress until the end of time. We're citizens of this divine and eternal realm yet continue to hold dual citizenship in the here and now. We scratch our heads over this kingdom, offering prayers about "building it up" through our efforts even as oracles from Scripture echo in our minds: "What kind of house can you build for *me*?" God's kingdom can't be constructed by human hands, and yet it can't be realized without putting our backs into its emergence. As Quaker mystic Rufus Jones says, "Few heresies are worse than the heresy that the kingdom of God is to come in a far-off sky, or by a sudden miracle. It is coming now as fast as we become children of God." There's no either/or in kingdom talk. It's always both/and.

## QOHELETH AND HIS POLARITIES

Is our friend Qoheleth way off base in his pendulum-swing perspective on reality? He dangles oppositional couplets of love and hate, war and peace, before our eyes and says: This is the world. This is how it is. Take it, accept it, because no better world is coming your way.

Jesus proclaims a better world *is* coming, is already here, coexisting alongside this one as a dream to be awakened, a possibility that can be chosen. Every hour plays an anthem to this new creation, if we but listen for it. We can be citizens of this new realm now because it's the kingdom of NOW, unfettered by past mistakes or future concerns. Now is kingdom's hour, since neither past nor future are in our hands. Now is the only moment in which you and I are free to choose, free to exercise our likeness to God in the power to decide.

Old philosopher Qoheleth has burned with love and hate. He's lived through war and peace just as we have, as each generation does. Some of us grow old and take on the shrug of inevitability betrayed in the couplets of Ecclesiastes 3. "Enjoy the good times, survive the bad times," we may advise the generations coming up behind us. "You can't do much to influence either." We may even peg Jesus for corroboration of our cynicism: Didn't he say there will always be poor? Aren't negative circumstances the inescapable consequences of a fallen world and in some sense destined to be?

Jesus is no cynic. Yet some wave his words about "inevitable poverty" as a flag hoisted in defense of compassion fatigue. I've heard Matthew 26:11 cited as absolution from charitable giving: we can't "fix" poverty, even Jesus says so! Yet look to Mark 14:7, which contains the full quotation Matthew only samples. There, Jesus says: "The poor you will always have with you, and whenever you wish you can do good to them, but you will not always have me." Those who first heard this saying would know Jesus is referencing a teaching in Deuteronomy 15:11: "The land will never lack for needy persons; that is why I command you: 'Open your hand freely to your poor and to your needy kin in your land.'"

Obviously, Jesus is not suggesting to Judas that assistance to the poor is irrelevant because poverty is inevitable. He references a commandment to assist the poor in every generation precisely because there are always those who need help. On the night in question, Jesus happens to be a man very much in need himself, facing what he knows is a death sentence.

The reality of good and evil is no excuse to relativize the two. Nor is it license to throw up our hands and let fate decide what will be. In the shadow of Qoheleth's well-drawn polarities, we're always choosers along a spectrum of the beneficial and the harmful. Our response to the cornucopia of choices between war and peace, for example, matters in ultimate ways. As the saying goes, war never determines who's right; it merely determines who's left. Pope John Paul II noted, "War is not inevitable. It is always a defeat for humanity." Pope Paul VI insisted that peace is more than the absence of war. What does choosing peace mean, and what will it cost?

Rufus Jones defines peacemaking as more than being personally nonviolent. "The pacifist stands for 'the fiery positive.' Pacifism is not a theory but a way of life. It is something you are and do." Martin Luther King Jr. pointed out that great military geniuses of history spoke of peace—but their words were empty in light of their actions. Alexander the Great, Julius Caesar, Charlemagne, and Napoleon all claimed to kill in the name of peace. "One day we must come to see that peace is not merely a distant goal we seek, but that it is a means by which we arrive at that goal," King wrote. "We must pursue peaceful ends through peaceful means."

King challenged us to consider the polarities involved: nonviolent coexistence or violent co-annihilation. He offered another spectrum of choice: chaos or community. Chaos, of course, is what God left behind in the creation of an orderly, purposeful, hopeful world. Community, the genuine unity of persons in pursuit of the common good, sounds like a hopeful way to restore some original goodness to this world.

Maybe Peter Seeger is a genius after all. Maybe his six-word addition to Ecclesiastes 3 is a vow worth taking: "I swear it's not too late."

*Lord of all possibility, how wonderfully you made us! Creatures from your hand, we have been endowed with divine likeness in our freedom to choose, to build, to create, and to love. We thank you for your confidence in us. We place our trust in your goodness, implicit in the world and waiting for its eternal restoration in your kingdom, which is coming, all the time. Amen.*

Life is an adventure. It's a graced encounter with the divine will, a discovery of kingdom coming in every moment. Or: it's a nightmare, a problem, a game, a battle. Reality has its polarities. We get to choose our place along the spectrum of what will be. Will we be heroes and saints, or safely self-serving? What story do we want our lives to tell? That we never did much harm, or that we contributed a world of good?

Some may determine, after reflecting on the polarities of Ecclesiastes 3, that Qoheleth presents a dramatic assessment of what life is about. Yes, he does. We may experience most days in a gentler stream of time like sands through the hourglass, or a breeze flowing through one window and out another. Time doesn't always feel like an endless duel between ways of love or hate. We may not feel life's urgent polarities as we pull our laundry out of the dryer or sort through junk mail.

Yet for mystics who see with kingdom eyes, human history is a drama of cosmic proportions. "The world is in flames!" Teresa of Ávila cried. "Now is not the time to be bothering God with trifles!" She couldn't abide her nuns praying conservative little prayers about personal backaches. Teresa saw the big picture with kingdom clarity and felt a state of emergency about the well-being of the world.

Most seasons of our lives may be routine or dull. But seasons will come in which we'll experience the world in flames—in dying, in mourning, when things break down or must be torn apart, when we weep and must speak out or perhaps scream out what's true and lacking and needed. In those seasons we will long for a mystical vision, but it may be too late to develop it. Now is the season for embracing the kingdom way of seeing! The time is coming when we'll be grateful we did.